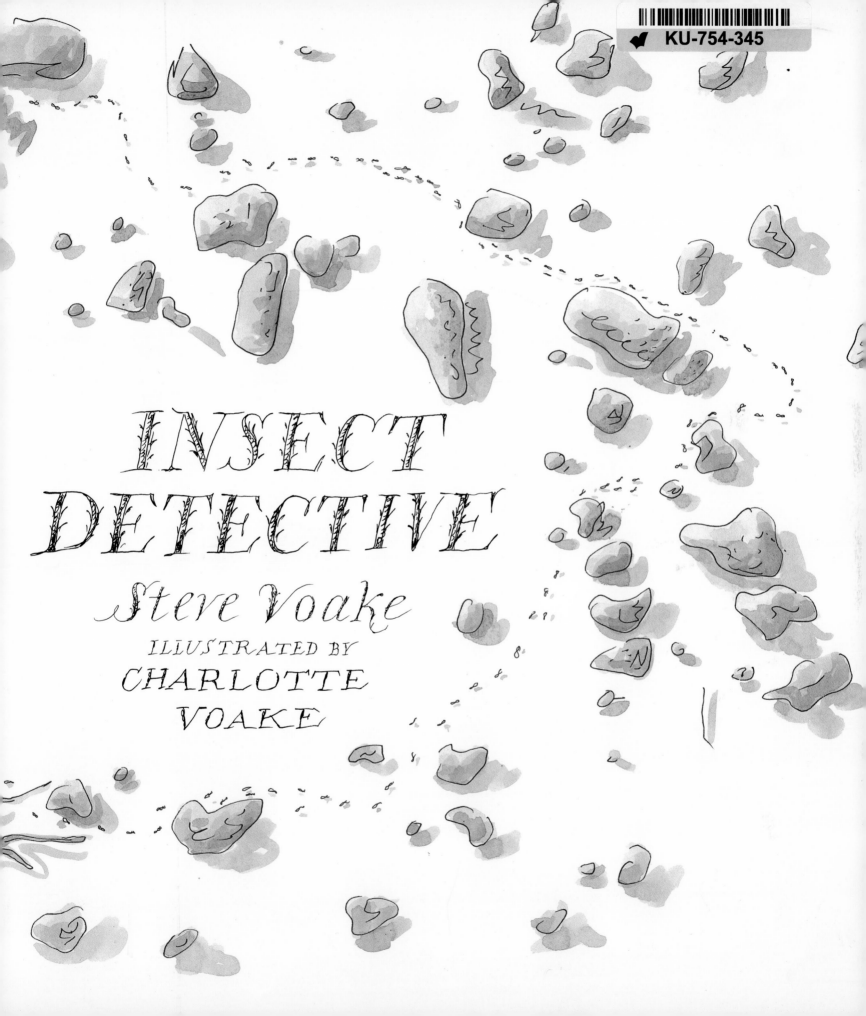

INSECT
DETECTIVE

Steve Voake

ILLUSTRATED BY
CHARLOTTE
VOAKE

RIGHT now, all around you,
thousands of insects are doing strange
and wonderful things.
But you can't always
see them straight away.

Sometimes you have to know
where to look...

First published 2009 by Walker Books Ltd
87 Vauxhall Walk, London SE11 5HJ

Text © 2009 Steve Voake
Illustrations © 2009 Charlotte Voake

The right of Steve Voake and Charlotte Voake
to be identified as author and illustrator respectively
of this work has been asserted by them in accordance
with the Copyright, Designs and Patents Act 1988

This book has been typeset in Godlike and Charlotte

Printed in China

British Library
Cataloguing in Publication Data:
a catalogue record for this book
is available from the
British Library

ISBN: 978-1-4063-1051-1
www.walker.co.uk

WALKER BOOKS
AND SUBSIDIARIES
LONDON · BOSTON · SYDNEY · AUCKLAND

For Tory
S. V.

THERE
ARE MORE
INSECTS LIVING
IN THE WORLD THAN ALL
THE OTHER ANIMALS PUT
TOGETHER – THAT'S ABOUT
200 MILLION INSECTS FOR EVERY
SINGLE PERSON!

LISTEN – just by the fence –
can you hear a scratching sound?
A wasp is scraping away at
the post with her strong jaws.
She's collecting wood.

She mixes it into a soft pulp
in her mouth and when she has
enough, she'll help the other wasps
build a nest out of paper.

WASPS
OFTEN COLLECT
DIFFERENT SORTS
OF WOOD, WHICH
MAKES THEIR NESTS
LOOK STRIPY – JUST
LIKE THE INSECTS
WHO MADE
THEM!

Not all kinds
of wasps live together,
but lots of them do.

INSECTS THAT LIVE TOGETHER ARE CALLED "SOCIAL INSECTS".

Ants *always* live together.

They usually make their nests underground.

Finding an ants' nest is easy:

FIRST find an ant ...

then follow it.

It might stop for a chat with some other

ants along the way (ants

can communicate

by touching their

antennae

together) ...

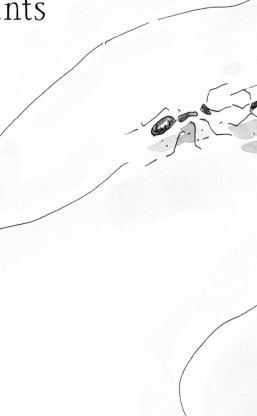

but after a while,
the ant will head for home
and you'll be able to
find out where it lives.

LIKE ALL INSECTS,
ANTS HAVE THREE MAIN
BODY PARTS.

THORAX

ABDOMEN

HEAD

Solitary bees live by themselves ("solitary" means alone). This female solitary bee is busy collecting food from the spring flowers. She'll store it in her tiny nest, ready for when her eggs hatch out.

ALL INSECTS START LIFE AS EGGS.

12

Solitary bees make their
nests in holes in the ground,
cracks in walls or in tiny
cavities that have been left
by other insects.

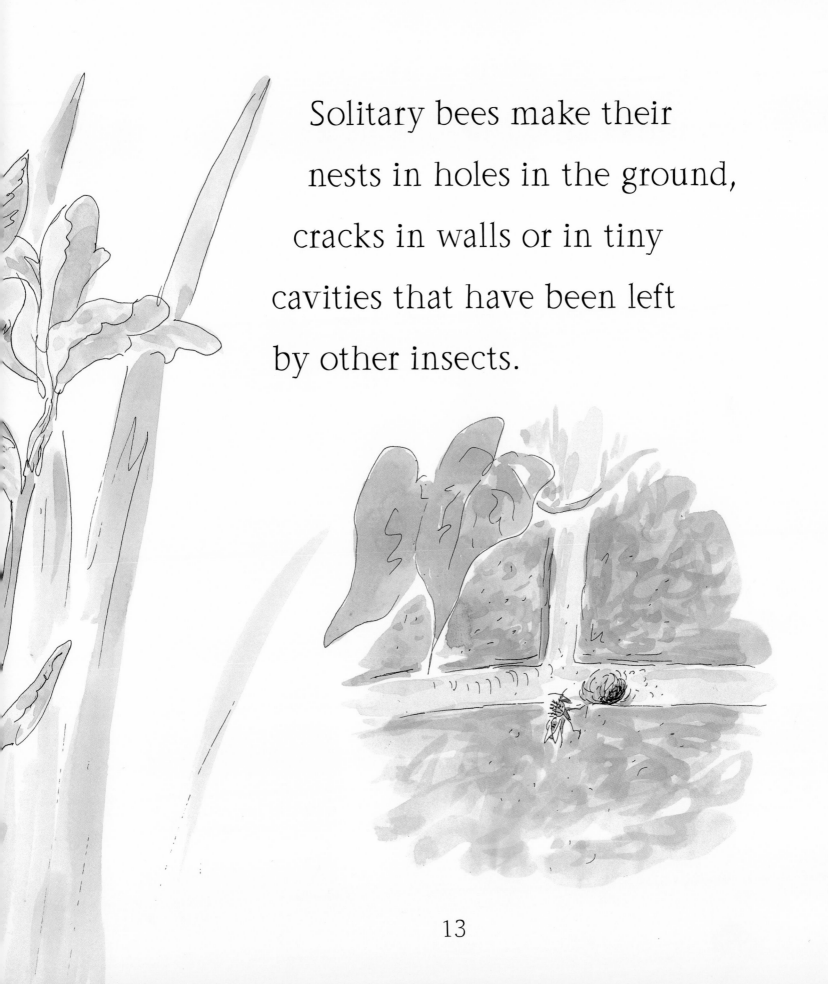

Plenty of animals like to eat insects for dinner. So some insects use camouflage to blend in with their surroundings.

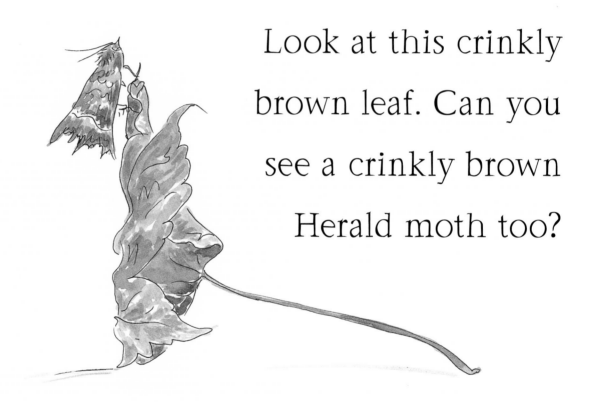

Look at this crinkly brown leaf. Can you see a crinkly brown Herald moth too?

They often rest in trees during the day so birds won't see them.

Insects have other
ways of hiding too.
See the squiggly
lines on these leaves?
They were made by
a leaf-miner caterpillar.
The leaf-miner protects
itself by living between
the top and bottom
layers of leaves –
a bit like
hiding in
a sandwich!

15

Lift up a stone ... you might see
an earwig scuttle out. They like
to hide in the damp and the dark.
The pincers on the tips of their abdomens
make them look rather fierce,
but don't worry – they're
completely harmless.

FEMALE EARWIGS ARE VERY GOOD MOTHERS. THEY WORK HARD TO KEEP THEIR EGGS CLEAN, TURNING AND WASHING THEM REGULARLY. WHEN THE YOUNG HATCH, THEIR MOTHERS BRING THEM FOOD UNTIL THEY'RE OLD ENOUGH TO LOOK AFTER THEMSELVES.

Of course, you *might* find some creatures under there which aren't insects:

spiders,

centipedes,

woodlice,

slugs ...

and once I found a
baby frog!

It's easy to
tell whether
something is
an insect or not.

All you have to do is count the legs.

1, 2, 3, 4, 5, 6 —

If it's got SIX legs, it's an insect.

If it hasn't ... it isn't!

If you're lucky, you
might even find
a violet ground beetle, gleaming in the
sunlight. It's like discovering a precious jewel!

But ground beetles aren't just lovely to look at, they're excellent hunters too. At night they go out hunting for slugs and snails, which makes gardeners very happy!

Perhaps the greatest insect
hunter of all is the dragonfly.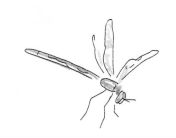
Even the name sounds fierce!
But don't worry – they won't come
chasing after you. Dragonflies are much
more interested in catching
things like bluebottles,
mosquitoes and
midges. Some will
even snatch a spider
from its web.

On summer days when the air is still, you can see their wings sparkling in the light as they hunt, twisting, diving and plucking flies from the air.

DRAGONFLIES ARE
FABULOUS FLIERS;
THEY HAVE TWO SETS OF
POWERFUL WINGS WHICH THEY CAN
USE TO HOVER,
CHANGE DIRECTION
AND EVEN TO FLY
BACKWARDS.

It's hard to believe they started life in the water ...

but dragonflies lay their eggs in ponds or slow-moving rivers, where they hatch out into small dragonfly "nymphs".

A nymph sheds its skin many times until it is fully grown. Finally it climbs out of the water and rests on the stem of a plant. As dawn breaks, its skin splits open and a beautiful dragonfly emerges, unfolding its wings and drying itself in the sun.

THE SPECIAL CHANGES THAT TAKE PLACE IN INSECTS' BODIES ARE CALLED "METAMORPHOSES". THEY HAPPEN IN DIFFERENT WAYS, AS INSECTS GROW FROM EGGS TO ADULTS.

Sometimes, when you think about these
strange and wonderful things – moths hiding,
ants talking, dragonflies changing –
it's hard to believe that they
could really be true.

But you don't have
to take my word
for it ...

all you have to do is open the door
and step outside.

BE AN INSECT DETECTIVE!

Find out which beetles live near you by burying a jam jar in the earth. Any beetles walking over the top during the night will fall in. But remember to check every morning and let them go when you have finished looking.

When it gets dark, put a camping light on a white sheet outside. This will attract moths and you will be able to get a really close look at them!

Leave a patch of nettles to grow in a corner of your garden – lots of caterpillars love to eat them. How many can you find?

Try making a place for solitary bees to live. Rinse out an empty tin can, put some glue (or melted wax) in the bottom and fill it with drinking straws. Then hang the can up with the straws pointing slightly downwards to prevent rain collecting in them. When spring arrives, you'll soon see a few bees coming along to investigate!

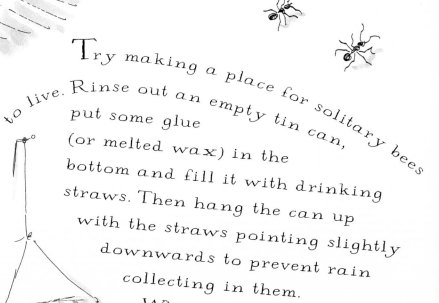

28

Flying can
be hard work
for bumble-bees.
If you see one crawling
around on the ground,
it may have run out
of energy.

Mix some sugar and water
in a teaspoon and give
it a drink –

it will soon be busy
amongst the flowers again!

Take a close look at
wooden tables, fences
or benches you see outside.
If they have tiny lines all
over them, you'll know
a wasp has
been there
before you.

In hot
thundery
weather, keep
an eye out
for swarming
ants. When the
temperature
is just right,
the young
queens will be
brought up to
the surface ready to
mate and fly away
to make new
colonies.

INDEX

Look up the pages
to find out about
all these insect things.
Don't forget to
look at both kinds
of word –

this kind

and

THIS KIND.